Golden Dawn
(*Poetry*)

By:
Barno Eshmurzayeva

© Taemeer Publications LLC
Golden Dawn *(Poetry)*
by: Barno Eshmurzayeva
Edition: August '2023
Publisher:
Taemeer Publications LLC (Michigan, USA / Hyderabad, India)

ISBN 978-93-5872-132-4

© Taemeer Publications

Book	:	Golden Dawn *(Poetry)*
Author	:	Barno Eshmurzayeva
Publisher	:	Taemeer Publications
Year	:	'2023
Pages	:	24
Title Design	:	*Taemeer Web Design*

Contents

1	I FOUND YOU HOMELAND!	5
2	NATURE	6
3	UMR	8
4	LIFE IS GOLD	10
5	THE SAVIOR SUN	11
6	MAN	12
7	CONSTITUTION	13
8	REMOTE ADDRESSES	14
9	TO UZBEKI GIRLS	15
10	MANGULIK PALACE	16
11	ZULFIYAHONIM	17
12	Institute in my life	18

I won't stop dreaming, don't you either! There is nothing wrong with a dream. I believe that these will make me a member of my country and people. After all, as President Shavkat Mirziyoyev said: "The most prestigious person in Uzbekistan should be a teacher."

1
I FOUND YOU HOMELAND!

From the sun's bright dew,

From the breath of nature

From the gentle breeze of the spring wind

I found you, Motherland!

I saw you

From bent purple leaves

From the anthills of Kizigan chuls

From the carok of the smiling gudak

I found you, Motherland!

I saw you.

Jumping from the fall of the playing arrow

From the mother's water that Allah says

Ko from the voice of the khafiz who sings

I found you, Motherland!

I saw you.

From a willow branch bent to streams,

Arik bhefrom the heat of the mint

From the blossoming bontar flower

I found you, Motherland!

I saw you.

2
NATURE

Full moon in the evening,

Do not caress your children.

The reflection of the stars is a stream,

He is breaking the silence.

Locusts are nocturnalhis daughter,

Gives pleasure to the heart.

Golddaylight- I ul Oshriek,

The wide world is full of moonsagon

Butterflies dance gracefully,

Theyib - theI laughed and watched.

Even if the night endsxplease

I can't leave, this is a strange thing.

All nature in motion,

But calm downhea human being.

It is written in this way,

a relaxing evening.

But the beautiful dawn,

The beautiful rays of the earth.

The sunset is unique,

More evening flowersg'little ones.

Even if I run, if I walkyesm void,

If I can't watch the night in the morning.

Enchant my feelings with poetry,

If I can't bring my heart to the morning.

3
UMR

The sun shines and vibrates in the sky,

Flowers - tomanadi purga.

Shabnam does magicg'smell the ubor

The butterfly opens the autumn and caressed.

At that moment, the light of autumn fades away,

Smallpox grew on the bosom of the leaves.

Kuvanib from such a sweet song

His wings flew around the sky.

The temperature of existence hits the day,

Nature drank its juice.

Running over the hills

To Bomar's delight, the night was full of flowers.

The sun shines towards the sunset,

For a butterfly, this is the world.

The light for the butterfly is every moment, every moment,

Mukaddas sanalur khar won time.

A poor creature in a day's life,

Does it feel like a vassal on Shabbat?

Don't the moments come back?

Ok, late for the funheavy

A breath I took in the sunset,

A beautiful butterfly has fallen from the world.

Come out soul! An ingrok, a sas was thrown!

Who did not hear from the reed bhelacquer

4
LIFE IS GOLD

Life is gold, life is goldxo!

It has pain and suffering.

He died by his command

At his command, the man stood up.

Time is the ruler of a person's life.

Time is the cure and cure for pain.

Better always bhewelcome

He is also happy, his reward is happiness.

Do you live happily? I don't know, secret

Do you live forever? Happiness or misfortune.

What secret is hidden under these waters,

In the eternal life toog'thank you

Your useful cocktail is worthy of praise,

This is the law of the world from time immemorial.

Let it be a century, or a million centuries,

A meaningful winning moment is preferable.

5
THE SAVIOR SUN

Khehna happy swinging bridegroom,

You never get tired of spreading light.

He is a good friend to the ground,

It shines over our heads.

Nature also gets light from it,

Here's how generous you are.

he sings so sweetly,

The hills are JUR to him.

The sunset to the golden dawn,

Spread your pure rays far and wide.

Sugartowardshe will come back

Share with us again g'du

6
MAN

Come on guys,

Kish came in again.

Beauty in nature,

Joy is a celebration.

The person has a strange charm,

In natureThere is magic

The silver man came in,

White blind in Hammayok.

I'm waiting with all my heart,

He is on duty when he arrives.

A monument from a man,

Kolar is a high stone blind.

7
CONSTITUTION

My duties and rights are embodied in you,

My happiness and my shame is my constitution.

I have faith and respect for Sam,

Take away my chief commissar - my constitution.

You are the pride and honor of Uzbekistan.

Acts of justice will fly from you.

You are the pure faith of my motherland,

You have a deep place in my heart.

8
REMOTE ADDRESSES

It's for those who take the imagination,

The skirts to distant destinations are bright.

The world is a stranger at will,

If a person is sought, he can be found.

Visit the meadows, steppes, meadows,

Life is complicated and passes quickly.

Drink water from my knowledgeheuntil

A beautiful, warm feeling of existence.

9
TO UZBEKI GIRLS

Hello, Kur girls of Uzbekistan,

You are honored with your beautiful birthday.

But, on your shoulderswhere is the roommate?

Where did you get the long, dark hair?

Loyalty and honor are only yours,

Ibo and Khayo are inherited from Momos.

Why don't you say it at home?

Are these qualities unfamiliar to you?

dar duppi sewn by gray flower moms,

Why is it not in your head today?

Usma's eyes are now in the kayak,

Will that day turn into a dream?

Let's get together girls

Let's not break the great tradition.

If we are the beauty of an independent Uzbek,

The world will recognize us.

10
MANGULIK PALACE

Painful Houses Beat My Heart,

Even if the heart doesn't beat, it stops.

Life is always like this,

Gok is a lamp, goji is like a night of darkness.

Man strives for eternity,

But who is too late for destiny?

Youth is courage, courage,

Utmish koshana is the palace of eternity.

11
ZULFIYAHONIM

How many FaM have you smoked Zulfiya Khanim,

You overcame everything and returned to life.

I call you my wing of the day,

Repeating your name.

God bless you faithful star,

How happy you were with him.

If you come back again, bear it.

He did not shed tearsg'your daughter

I will sleep with my heart,

Verses reveal secrets one by one.

You tell me laughing

"This life is bitter, this world is sweet!"

Gol Ukisam Urtanar my heart,

Sometimes happiness is more than happiness.

In the steps you take, you walkhein l

May your prayers always be with us!

Institute in my life

"My Dear children! Never forget that our people, our Motherland, expect great things from you! It is the greatest happiness in the world to fully justify the country's high trust and hope, to be worthy of it. May such an honor be granted to all of you", - these are the words of our honorable President Shavkat Mirziyoyev expressing his confidence in the youth of Uzbekistan.

... Finally, I also found a small path to achieve this great happiness. And now I am taking one step at a time to get out on a wide and clear path through this path. I believe that my destination is a bright future, a destiny close to the destiny of my country... The place I am walking now is my favorite institution - Jizzakh State Pedagogical Institute.

Admission to higher education institution, news of being recommended for studentship, celebrating it with parents, friends, peers...

It was different with me. Kamina joined the institute after I became a parent of two children. "Why is it so late?" you say I graduated from school and college with honors. I became the owner of a beautiful red diploma. I applied to the institute for the first time in 2010. But I could not pass. My heart full of dreams, to be a selfless teacher, to teach children - all my intentions fell into the abyss, and I fell into a depression that I could not get out of there for a lifetime. This depression followed me during the three years of exams. I looked everywhere for the reason. Maybe I was born in a poor family with eleven children, my poor parents were short-handed,

I didn't get tutored in the city like my friends, or if not, it was because of the entrance exams that were rampant at that time. injustices are the reason for this. I didn't blame myself for being a child. I don't have enough determination.

I have absolutely no right to blame my parents. Because I learned love for books from my father. The gratitude was that my father had a chest of books. We children grew up reading these books. My mother was a nurse. But they could not work more than us from household chores. They became devoted mothers.

When I took pride of place at the regional and republic levels in the contests, and my poetry book was published, my mother flew to the seventh heaven, saltiness. "My daughter will study in institutes, brighten my face, become a scientist," they boasted to the neighboring women.

"I'm sorry, mother, your dreams have come true," I cried, entering a big fortress called "marriage". I have lost my ways in life. I decided to be an obedient daughter-in-law, a worthy wife. Because I inherited selflessness from my mother.

However, the candle of my dreams did not go out, as I faced the trials of life, this candle flame kept burning my heart. I became a loving mother. More dedication…

Finally, my children went to school. It's not just a mother's joy, but at the very least, I'm mentoring my own children!

I taught them every day with all my heart and read books. One day, my daughter suddenly said something that "awakened" me: "Why aren't you a teacher, my dear!" Be our teacher tomorrow, Farangiz is my friend's moon doctor, the only one is a teacher!" My son went to join him.

From that day, all kinds of thoughts started running in my mind. In fact, my children also want to be proud that their mother is a teacher. In order for them to become educated, worthy children who serve the Motherland, I must also be educated. Our President keeps repeating: "Parents play a big role in the spiritual development of our children."

Even if my husband is not educated, they are understanding people. They said, "You should study for the future of our children." We lived separately from my in-laws. But my father-in-law was the head of the farm. Therefore, in addition to domestic work, there were also field works. My parents said, "Don't second-guess your in-laws' words, don't look them in the face!" His advice was always under my ear. I have to do something. After thinking about it, I decided not to tell them yet. They are not bad people. Anyway, I was shocked.

As they say, "Holva is not enough," I knew that I would not pass the exams without preparation. It was tested in the experiment. I couldn't make a mistake now. I found a tutor at school. Like my brother, he is a conscientious young man with excellent knowledge. "Sister, come, you don't even need money, just go to school, you're like my sister." God, may his career be great! I became applicant friends with girls twelve years younger than me. But among them I became a young girl. We used to debate, answer questions, and do tests about my favorite subject of language and literature.

But it was not easy. As they say, study, livelihood, children. I can say that I forgot what sleep is, I didn't walk, I ran. My children, my eyes... If I read a book until midnight, they fall asleep next to me, with their heads in their notebooks. Sometimes I feel sorry for them, sometimes I am happy. They do not miss the book. "A bird does what it sees in its nest." Oh, so many truths.

In the morning, I do household chores, run to the field, come home in the middle of the night, take my books and notebooks and run to school. It's hot because it's summer. I'm at school until work starts again in the afternoon. Bless my teacher, they understood me and adjusted the class time to my time. They also taught other subjects themselves. Because I could not go anywhere else to study.

Many people in our village knew that I was preparing. Some of them were benevolent, while others said, "If you are a mother of two children, now there is a way to study." So what's wrong? Our grandfathers said, "Seek knowledge from the cradle to the grave." The President said, "Let our children be educated" and created as many conditions and privileges as possible. Especially to women.

So, the exams were passed and the results were announced. I became a student chasing after my dreams. Thank you God! My mother, my happy mother... they cried. Cry, mother, cry if I made you cry from joy. My father-in-law, who was shocked, was happy that my daughter-in-law had started studying, and it was surprising. "The teacher came out of us," he boasts to those around him. In our village, there are many brides who want to study, but are afraid of it. Sparks of hope shone in their hearts. There are also mothers-in-law who want to educate their daughters-in-law. Parents started speaking as an example to their children. It was a special honor. I repeated only one sentence to them:

"Movement, tireless work, now there are all conditions,

Jizzakh State Pedagogical Institute. Now I am studying in this institute, under the hands of enthusiastic, kind and knowledgeable teachers. I have fellow students who are sincere and eager for knowledge. There are so many things I don't know and need to learn that I want to learn them as soon as possible. Looking at the conditions and books in the library of the institute, I feel as if I fell into a magical world, and all this is a great wealth for me. I consider it my duty to have this treasure, to be a worthy child of my country, which blessed me as a student, and to pass on the jewels of knowledge that I have to future generations.

My beloved institute, dear teachers, maybe they will be surprised to see a first-year student of my age, but I am happy. The path leading to my great goal in life started from the institute.

I won't stop dreaming, don't you either! There is nothing wrong with a dream. I believe that these will make me a member of my country and people. After all, as President Shavkat Mirziyoyev said: "The most prestigious person in Uzbekistan should be a teacher."

www.ingramcontent.com/pod-product-compliance
Lightning Source LLC
LaVergne TN
LVHW021240080526
838199LV00088B/5435